CONTENTS

ROARING ROCKETS

he Moon is a long way from Earth, but at night it can seem very close. For thousands of years people looked up at the Moon and wondered what it would be like to go there. This book tells the story of how people finally found a way to travel there, and how a human first walked on the Moon.

▶ A German V-2 rocket, one of the first rocket-powered bombs, is launched during the Second World War.

SHOOTING SHELLS

In 1865, the French writer Jules Verne wrote a book called *From The Earth To The Moon*. He described how giant shells could be fired to the Moon from a huge cannon. The shells would contain the first Moon explorers (see opposite).

This 1934 space suit doesn't look comfortable or safe! It was never tested in space.

In the 1930s, scientists in Germany, the USA and the Soviet Union started carrying out experiments with rockets. The first rockets were not very powerful. They could only reach heights of a few hundred metres.

During the Second World War, from 1939 to 1945, people found a new use for rockets. Germany began making rockets that could travel for hundreds of kilometres. They used them to launch bombs at England.

After the Second World War, the German scientists who had made these deadly rockets went to work in the USA. But for a long time the Americans did not realize just how important rockets would become.

An illustration from Jules Verne's book *From The Earth To The Moon.*

DAREDEVIL DOG

▲ Laika the Soviet space dog in her capsule, not long before she became the first living creature in space.

During the 1950s, there were two countries that were much more powerful than the rest. These were the USA and the Soviet Union. They were so powerful that they were known as superpowers.

The two superpowers were great enemies. They competed with each other in weapons, politics, sport and science. They also began an amazing space race to see who could explore the farthest in space.

SPUTNIK SPOTTERS

Many American children became *Sputnik* spotters. They stared into the sky at night, and tried to spot the Soviet Union's satellites as they passed overhead.

▶ **This is a drawing of the Soviet Union's *Sputnik 1* satellite.**

In October 1957, the Soviet Union launched the world's first satellite, called *Sputnik*. A satellite is a machine that flies through space, travelling around Earth in a big loop, or orbit. *Sputnik* flew over the USA once every hour. Americans were terrified. They thought the Soviet Union might attack them from space.

Soon the Soviet Union was even farther ahead in the space race. It launched *Sputnik 2*, a satellite containing a female dog named Laika. She spent ten days in orbit around Earth. The Soviet Union was the first country to put a living creature in space.

▶ **Russian astronauts with their space dog, testing out their space suits.**

MERCURY MAGIC

The USA tried to launch its own satellite called *Explorer* in December 1957. The launch was a disaster. The rocket that was supposed to fire the satellite into space exploded before it left the ground!

The USA was a long way behind in the space race. Then two things happened. An organization called NASA was formed to run the USA's space projects. Also, John F Kennedy became president of the USA. Kennedy set NASA a target. He said it should land a man on the Moon and return him safely to Earth by 1970.

▲ The seven Mercury astronauts in their space suits.

▼ President Kennedy calls for the USA to send a man to the Moon by 1970.

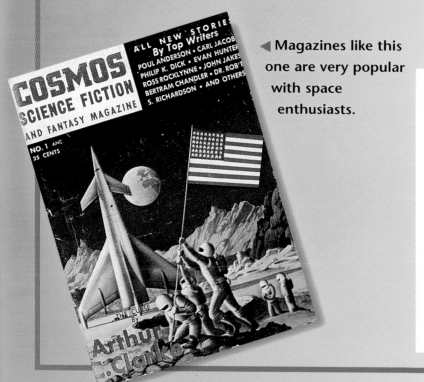

◄ Magazines like this one are very popular with space enthusiasts.

NASA began the Mercury Project, with the aim of getting a human into space. Seven astronauts were chosen to fly spacecraft for the project, and they quickly became heroes. People thought the astronauts were very brave, and they wanted to know everything about them. The seven men appeared on television, and in newspapers and magazines. Americans were becoming more and more interested in space.

SPACE CRAZE

By the early 1960s, the USA had gone crazy about space. There were space programmes on television, space records in the music charts and even space colouring books!

▲ *Explorer I,* moments before it exploded on the launch pad.

SPACEMAN

The Soviet Union began sending up spacecraft called probes to take photographs of the Moon in 1959. Probes send back information automatically, so they do not need anybody on board. But the Soviet Union also had plans to send a man into space.

▼ The launch of *Vostok I* from Baikonur in the Soviet Union at 9.07 am on 12 April 1961. The astronaut Yuri Gagarin was on board.

On 12 April 1961, a spacecraft called *Vostok I* was launched from the Soviet Union. On board was an astronaut named Yuri Gagarin. He soared 327 kilometres above Earth's surface and into space. Gagarin circled the world before landing back in the Soviet Union.

In the USA, people were shocked when they heard of Gagarin's flight. The Soviet Union had won all the first parts of the space race. It had launched the first satellite and put the first living creature in space. Now it had put the first human in space. There was only one race left to win – the race to put a human on the Moon.

▲ Celebrations in the Soviet Union after Yuri Gagarin became the first man to visit space.

▶ Alan Shepard after his return to Earth, with the *Freedom 7* capsule behind him.

SPACEWALK

The USA had some catching up to do in the space race. It began an important programme called the Gemini Project.

The Gemini Project had three goals. First, an astronaut had to make a spacewalk, by going outside his spacecraft during a flight. Second, astronauts had to show they could stay alive in space for a long time. Third, two spacecraft had to link up, or dock, in space. If they could do these three things, the Americans believed they would be almost ready to send a human to the Moon and back.

▲ America's *Gemini 6* spacecraft about to dock with *Gemini 7*.

WOLF WALK

The first ever spacewalk was made by Soviet astronaut Alexei A Leonov in March 1965. But when his spacecraft, *Voskhod 2*, returned to Earth it landed in a lonely forest. Leonov had to fight off hungry wolves before he was rescued!

In June 1966, astronaut Ed White left a spacecraft called *Gemini 4* and made a spacewalk. The project's next spacecraft, *Gemini 5*, orbited Earth 120 times. This was the longest space flight yet, and it showed that humans could stay alive in space. Finally, the spacecraft *Gemini 6* and *Gemini 7* docked while in orbit. The Gemini Project had achieved its goals.

▲ Astronaut Ed White floats in space during his spacewalk. He used a rocket gun to move himself forwards.

Amazing Apollo

NASA started to make plans for the journey to the Moon. It began a project called Apollo. The aim of the Apollo Project was to build a spacecraft that could carry a human safely to the Moon and back.

▼ NASA planned to land astronauts on the Moon in a lunar module.

Moon

Command module orbits Moon

After orbiting Earth, command module and lunar module head towards Moon

Rocket takes off and separates

Earth

Lunar module lands on Moon

NASA came up with a special plan. A giant rocket would power the spacecraft towards the Moon. As it used up its fuel, parts of the rocket would fall away. Finally, only two parts of the spacecraft would be left. One part, called the lunar module, would land on the Moon. The other part, called the command module, would stay in orbit around the Moon. Then it would dock with the lunar module and carry the astronauts safely back to Earth.

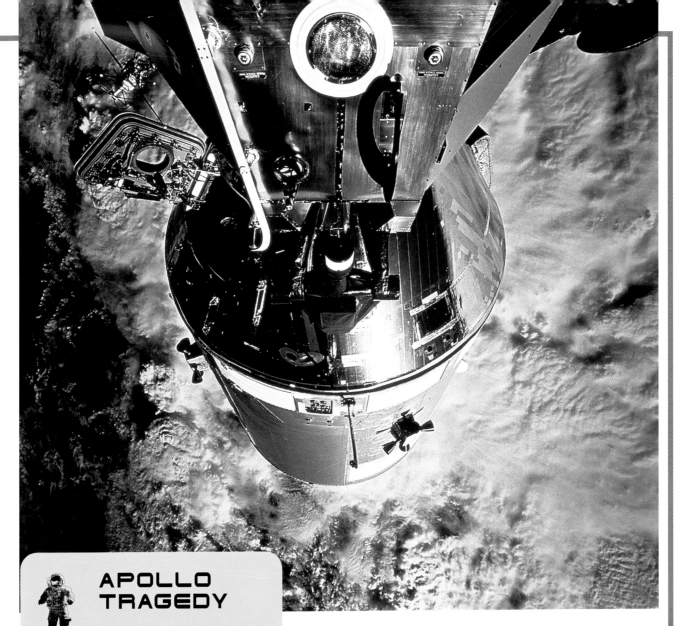

APOLLO TRAGEDY

The Apollo project had a very bad start. The first spacecraft, *Apollo I*, began practising its launch. Suddenly there was an explosion. Tragically, the three astronauts on board were all killed.

▲ *Apollo 9*'s lunar module docks with the command module in 1968.

Scientists began building a giant rocket, called *Saturn 5*. It was tested in November 1967. This would carry the Apollo spacecraft into space. Work also began on a lunar module that could land safely on the Moon. The USA was almost ready to send an astronaut to the Moon.

INTO ORBIT

The USA took the lead in the space race on Christmas Eve 1968. A spacecraft called *Apollo 8* went into orbit around the Moon. The astronauts on board sent back a message: 'From the crew of *Apollo 8*... good night, good luck, a merry Christmas, and God bless all of you... on the good Earth.'

The Soviet Union carried on exploring the Moon by sending up probes. Scientists had sent up 14 probes by the time *Apollo 8* circled the Moon.

▲ The Soviet Union's *Luna 9* unmanned Moon probe, which landed on the Moon in 1966.

▼ An Apollo astronaut practises lifting equipment while wearing his space suit.

Some of the probes landed on the Moon. Others passed by and carried on into space. The probes gathered lots of information, but still no human had stood on the Moon's surface.

The American spacecraft *Apollo 9* and *Apollo 10* both carried a lunar module into space for tests in March and May of 1969. When they came back to Earth, their astronauts reported that the module worked perfectly. Everything was now ready for *Apollo 11* to make the first landing on the Moon.

▼ *Apollo 9's* **command module in orbit around Earth.**

MARVELLOUS MARBLE

The *Apollo 8* astronauts were the first people to see Earth from space. It must be strange to see your own planet from such a distance. One of the astronauts said it looked like a 'big, blue marble'.

LUNAR LANDING

Early in the morning of 16 July 1969, *Apollo 11* took off from Cape Canaveral in Florida, USA. On board were the astronauts Neil Armstrong, Buzz Aldrin and Mike Collins. Over a million people were gathered at Cape Canaveral to watch as the massive rocket blasted off. Millions more saw the lift-off on television.

MOTOR MOUTH

Scientists kept an eye on *Apollo 11* from a centre in Houston, Texas, USA called Mission Control. During the Moon landing, the astronauts were talked to by a man at Mission Control called Charlie Duke. He talked so much that someone nudged him and said: 'Shut up and let them land!'

▶ *Apollo 11* blasts-off from its launch pad at Cape Canaveral, Florida.

18

Apollo 11 took three days to travel to the Moon. When it arrived, Armstrong and Aldrin climbed into the lunar module, which was called *Eagle*. Collins pushed a button inside the command module, and the *Eagle* broke away. Armstrong and Aldrin were on their way to the surface of the Moon.

Close to the surface, Armstrong looked down at where they had planned to land. He saw that it was too rocky. The *Eagle's* fuel was running out. But Armstrong flew on, searching for a good landing spot. At the last moment he saw one. *Eagle* landed with its fuel tanks nearly empty.

▼ The lunar module *Eagle*, separated from the command module, floats above the surface of the Moon.

A Giant Leap

Millions of people watched on televisions around the world as Neil Armstrong opened the door of the *Eagle*. For thousands of years, people had looked up at the Moon and wondered what it would be like to stand on it. Now, they were about to find out.

▲ Buzz Aldrin comes out of *Eagle* and begins to climb down the ladder to the surface of the Moon.

◄ Armstrong, Aldrin and the American flag stand in the sunlight on the Moon.

Armstrong stepped through the door, and climbed down *Eagle's* ladder. Then he put one foot on the surface of the Moon, and said: 'That's one small step for man, one giant leap for mankind.'

Aldrin joined Armstrong on the Moon shortly afterwards. Gravity (the force that keeps our feet on the ground) on the Moon is six times weaker than it is on Earth, so the astronauts felt very light. They were able to take giant steps, covering two metres in a single leap!

The astronauts took out an American flag, and planted it on the Moon's surface. This was the moment the USA had been waiting for. Their flag, and not that of the Soviet Union, was the first to be placed there. They had won the race to the Moon!

FANTASTIC FOOTPRINTS

As they walked about, the astronauts made footprints in the dusty surface of the Moon. There is no air on the Moon to blow the dust away, so these footprints will last for thousands of years!

SPLASHDOWN!

Apollo 11 returned to Earth on 24 July 1969. The spacecraft entered Earth's atmosphere at a speed of 39 750 km/h. Because it was travelling so fast, it was glowing with heat!

Parachutes opened to slow *Apollo 11* down. By the time it hit the surface of the Pacific Ocean, it was moving much more slowly. The astronauts had travelled 800 000 km. They made their splashdown just 20 km from the ship that was to pick them up.

▼ The three astronauts being collected from the command module after splashdown.

Mike Collins in the command module.

ALL ALONE

The pilot of the command module, Mike Collins, never walked on the Moon. But he did some special things of his own. As he travelled around the Moon, he spent time all alone on its far side. He was farther from Earth than any other person.

President Nixon was waiting to greet the astronauts. But he was not allowed to shake their hands. Scientists were worried that the astronauts might have brought a horrible Moon disease back to Earth with them!

The astronauts were kept alone for three weeks. When they were allowed out, they found that they had become heroes. Parties and parades were held to celebrate the amazing achievement of the first men on the Moon.

▼ Armstrong, Aldrin and Collins became heroes across America. This photo shows a ticker-tape parade in New York city.

SPACE STATION

▼ The space shuttle is used to carry astronauts and equipment to the International Space Station.

The amazing race had been won. Humans had reached the Moon. But *Apollo 11* was not the last spacecraft to carry people to the Moon.

Between 1969 and 1972, Apollo spacecraft carried astronauts to the Moon six times. In 1972, the final mission to the Moon, *Apollo 17*, left a plaque on the Moon's surface. It read: 'Here man completed his first exploration of the Moon, December 1972.' No human has stood on the Moon since.

▼ The American space shuttle docks with the Russian space station *Mir*.

▲ The International
Space Station.

But people have not stopped exploring space. Scientists still send probes to distant planets. They also build huge spacecraft called space stations, such as the International Space Station, where astronauts can live and work for months at a time.

But the Soviet Union and the USA no longer fight over space. Instead, different countries work together to study the amazing moons, stars and planets of space.

 SUPER
STATION

The largest project in space is the International Space Station. This huge structure allows Russia (part of the former Soviet Union), the USA and 14 other countries to work together. Scientists will carry out experiments in the space station that are impossible to do on Earth.

▲ US Senator John Glenn, one of America's first astronauts, before he returned to space in 1998.

SPACE-RACE FACTS

Unlucky brake

Yuri Gagarin became the first man in space in 1961. But in 1995 secret notes about his flight were found. They showed that his spacecraft almost crashed on its way back to Earth, because of a problem with its braking rocket.

First females

After his amazing flight, Yuri Gagarin went on to become the training director of the first-ever programme to train female astronauts.

Space professor

Neil Armstrong earned his pilot's licence on his 16th birthday! He later worked as a fighter-pilot. When he retired from NASA in 1971, he became a professor of engineering at the University of Cincinnati.

Monkey business

Scientists were worried that humans would not be able to stay alive when travelling in a rocket at amazing speeds. So, between 1948 and 1952 scientists in the USA carried out tests. They flew monkeys on rockets that had been captured from Germany.

Star laws

There are many laws in space. One of the most important is the 1967 Outer Space Treaty. This says that the Moon and all other moons, stars and planets are free to be explored by people from all countries.

◄ Werner von Braun, one of the first rocket scientists.

Rocket man

Many of the scientists who worked on rockets for the USA after the Second World War came from Germany. Werner von Braun, one of the most important scientists, had worked on the building of rocket-powered bombs for the German leader Adolf Hitler.

Mighty *Mir*

In 1986, the Soviet Union launched a space station called *Mir* (which means 'peace' in Russian). *Mir* finally came back to Earth in March 2001, after 14 years in space.

Good Goddard!

The first rockets launched in the USA were built by a famous American named Robert Goddard. He was once asked by the State of Massachusetts not to set off his rockets within the state. The rockets were thought to be too dangerous!

Rocket to riches

In 1960, the widow of Robert Goddard accepted $1 000 000. In return, the US government was allowed to use the rockets he had invented in its space programme.

▶ **Valentina Tereshkova, who became the first woman in space in 1963.**

Valentina's day

The first woman in space was Valentina Tereshkova. She travelled into space on 16 June 1963, aboard a spacecraft called *Vostok 6*. She returned to Earth three days later.

Shuttle Ride

The USA did not get a woman into space until 20 years after the Soviets! The first American woman in space was Sally Ride, who flew aboard the space shuttle in 1983.

Space-Race Words

Apollo
Apollo was the third programme set up by the USA to explore space. The *Apollo 11* spacecraft carried the first people ever to reach the Moon.

astronaut
Someone who travels into space.

atmosphere
The group of gases around the surface of a planet. Near to Earth's surface, the atmosphere is made up mainly of nitrogen. Higher up, there are other gases such as ozone.

automatically
Working by itself, without the need for human control. Space probes travel and automatically send back information, such as recordings and photographs. So they do not need a pilot.

▶ The *Eagle* lunar module.

command module
The part of an Apollo spacecraft that stayed in orbit around the Moon while the lunar module visited the Moon's surface.

dock
Join spacecraft together in space.

Gemini
Gemini was the second programme set up by the USA to explore space. The first American spacewalk was made from a spacecraft called *Gemini 4*.

gravity
Any object has a natural force called gravity, which pulls things towards it.

The gravity of Earth is what holds us all on the ground, and stops us floating off into space!

lift-off
The moment when a rocket leaves the ground, also called blast-off.

lunar
Lunar simply means anything to do with the Moon.

lunar module
The part of an *Apollo* spacecraft that visited the surface of the Moon and then brought the astronauts back to the command module.

Mercury
Mercury was the first programme set up by the USA to explore space.

Mission Control
The American command centre on Earth that runs space flights. For the Apollo space flights, Mission Control was in Houston, Texas, USA.

NASA
NASA stands for National Aeronautics and Space Agency, and was formed in the USA in 1958. Before NASA existed, both the US Army and the US Navy had their own rocket programmes. NASA combined these programmes, and helped the USA to catch up with the Soviet Union in the space race.

▲ The *Skylab* space station orbiting Earth.

orbit
The path that a smaller object travels through space around a larger one. For example, the Moon travels in orbit around Earth. The Moon is held in this orbit by the pull of gravity from Earth. Spacecraft such as satellites can also be sent into orbit around moons, stars and planets.

politics
Different ways of running countries and forming governments.

probe
A spacecraft without anyone on board, which explores distant moons and planets. Both the USA and the Soviet Union have sent many probes into space. Some are still travelling through space today, sending back information about the objects they pass.

rocket
A powerful engine that burns fuel, and releases a jet of gas that moves the engine forwards very quickly. Rockets are used to carry bombs and spacecraft to their target. Powerful rockets are needed to fire spacecraft away from the pull of Earth's gravity.

satellite
A satellite is a machine that flies through space, travelling around a large object such as Earth or the Moon in a big loop, or orbit.

space station
A large satellite in space, on which astronauts can live and work for long periods of time.

Sputnik
Sputnik means 'travelling companion' in Russian. It was the name given to three satellites from the Soviet Union launched in 1957–8.

superpower
A superpower is a country that is much more powerful than most other countries. During the space race, the Soviet Union and the USA were known as the world's two superpowers.

Soviet Union
A huge country in eastern Europe, which was formed in 1922 with Russia at its heart. In 1991, the Soviet Union broke up into much smaller states. Even so, Russia is still one of the world's most important nations.

SPACE-RACE PROJECTS

▶ The Moon, seen from space.

MOON LANDING REPORT

Write a newspaper article about the Moon landing. To write your report, use the information in this book and in other books and websites. You could write your report in one of three ways:

1. Pretend you are an American reporter. Write an article telling the people of the USA how two Americans have just become the first people on the Moon.

2. Pretend you are a news reporter from the Soviet Union. Your job is to tell people how the Americans have landed on the Moon. But you must also remind them of all the things the Soviet Union has done in space.

3. Imagine you are an alien visiting from another galaxy.

What do you think of the Moon landing? Remember that such a visitor would have travelled from a lot further away than the Moon!

MOON SPOTTER

Try to find a book that includes a map of the Moon. You might be able to find one that shows the different areas where the Moon landings took place. You could also look on the Internet to see if there are any maps of the Moon.

Now you need a telescope! Your school might have one. There might even be a local club for astronomers, people who like to study the stars. Ask about these things at your school. On a clear night and using a telescope, you can actually see some of the different areas where the Moon landings took place.

SPACE RACE ON THE INTERNET

If you have access to the Internet, you will be able to track down some more information about the space race. Try looking up these websites to start you off:

NASA website
www.nasa.gov
Some of the best websites about space belong to NASA. Among them is a site where you can read the information that was given to newspapers before the *Apollo 11* mission. This might be useful if you have chosen to be an American reporter for the Moon landing report project.

Kennedy Space Center
www.ksc.nasa.gov
The Kennedy Space Center, from which the Apollo flights were launched, has pages all about history. It also tells you what is happening at the Kennedy Space Center today.

NASA Human Spaceflight
www.spaceflight.nasa.gov
The International Space Center homepage is also the homepage for the space shuttle.

BBC Online
www.bbc.co.uk
The BBC has a good short section on the Moon landings on its news website. Try to find the quotes from Charlie Duke, who was at Mission Control during the Moon landing.

You can search for other sites on the space race using any search engine. Try typing in keywords such as 'rocket', 'Gemini' or 'Apollo'.

▶ **Buzz Aldrin walking on the Moon.**

INDEX

LOOK FOR THE ASTRONAUT

Look out for boxes like this with an astronaut in the corner. They contain extra information and amazing space buster facts and figures.

Produced by
Monkey Puzzle Media Ltd,
Gissing's Farm, Fressingfield,
Suffolk IP21 5SH, UK

First published in Great Britain
in 2002 by
 Chrysalis Children's Books
64 Brewery Road,
London N7 9NT

Copyright © Chrysalis Books PLC
2002

Paperback edition first published
in 2003

A Belitha Book

Designer: Tim Mayer
Editor: Jason Hook
Consultant: Steve Parker

ISBN 1 84138 366 X (hb)
ISBN 1 84138 771 1 (pb)

British Library Cataloguing in
Publication Data for this book is
available from the British Library.

Printed in Hong Kong
10 9 8 7 6 5 4 3 2 1 (hb)
10 9 8 7 6 5 4 3 2 1 (pb)

Acknowledgements
We wish to thank the following individuals and organizations for their help and assistance and for supplying material in their collections: Camera Press 4; Corbis 3 (Bettmann), 8 bottom right (Bettmann), 9, (Bettmann), 11 bottom (Dean Conger), 12 (NASA/Roger Ressmeyer), 17 (NASA), 22 (Bettmann), 26 (Hulton-Deutsch); Mary Evans Picture Library 5 bottom; MPM Images front cover, back cover bottom left, back cover bottom right, 18, 20 top, 24 main image, 25 top, 28, 29, 30, 31; NASA back cover top, 1, 8 top, 13, 19, 20 bottom, 21, 23 bottom; Rex Features 10, 24 inset; Science and Society Picture Library 8 bottom left (The Clarkives), 15 (NASA), 16 bottom (NASA); Science Photo Library 7 top (David A Hardy); Topham Picturepoint 5 top, 6, 7 bottom, 11 top (Tass), 16 top (Novosti), 23 top, 25 bottom, 27. Artwork by Alex Pang.

▼ This odd-looking vehicle was designed to land humans on the Moon.

▶ Moon explorers return to Earth. They are dressed in special suits to keep humans safe from Moon germs.

S P A C E R A C E
S P A C RS TERS

Paul Mason

Chrysalis Children's Books